D0292387

STRATAGEM

Simple, Effective Strategic Planning for Your Business and Your Life

by

Sandy Manson, Jay Nisberg and Gary Shamis

with Kristen Hampshire

A Smart Business Network Inc. imprint

Published by:
Smart Business Network
835 Sharon Dr., Suite 200
Westlake, OH 44145

Printed in the United States of America

Contributing writer: Kristen Hampshire
Editor: Randy Wood
Cover design: Amanda Horvath and Stacy Vickroy
Interior design: Kaelyn Hrabak and Randy Wood

ISBN: 978-0-9889622-6-2

Library of Congress Control Number: 2013942783

Contents

Acknowledgements

To all the great people at Johnston Carmichael I have been lucky enough to join on what continues to be an amazing journey. And to my wife Barbara, my best friend and supporter.

SM

I want to thank and acknowledge the women in my life without whose help I would never have found the time or motivation to help write this book. First, I must thank my wife Sally Ann. Her vision and strength these past two years during her courageous and successful fight with breast cancer became my inspiration to get up every day and do what I do. She looked into the *eye of the tiger*, showed courage and helped me understand that attitude is everything. I want to thank my daughter Alicia Michelle Nisberg for always "calling it as she sees it." Her candor kept me focused and helped me get beyond the small stuff. Thanks to my step-daughter Brooke Erin Marcogliese for her artistic push on the cover of this book. A very special thank you to my friend and assistant Barbara Hudson, without whose guidance I'd never get to the right place on time, and her ever-present help to make the right decisions. Finally, thank you to Sally Ann's sister, Jackie Marcelli, who was at Sally's side through every surgery and every treatment during her fight with breast cancer. Jackie's advice was greatly appreciated but her love for family is even more valuable. Thank you, ladies, for who you are and what you mean to me.

JN

To my clients and partners who allowed me to help them with Stratagem. And to my family who allowed me the time — thanks Ben, Nicole, Melissa, Eli and Mar.

GS

Foreword

I recently returned from a trip to Montana where senior management from our firm completed our second Stratagem session in less than three years. As I reflect on the most recent Stratagem session and look to our future, I feel compelled to look back as well. How did our business get to where we are today and how do we stay on track in order to get to where we want to be?

While many factors have influenced our company and its evolution, I can't ignore Dec. 31, 2008. It was New Year's Eve and I was waiting in line at a popular restaurant in the small town in which I live when a gentleman approached me. He said he had been following a somewhat controversial real estate redevelopment deal I was involved with in the newspaper. He expressed his support of our efforts and, as a professional in business management, he was interested in learning more about me, a mere 36-year-old kid who, along with a partner had just ventured out on our own. He seemed quite focused on the fact that I was what he referred to as *a change agent*. Ultimately, the gentleman gave me his card and suggested that I call him to set up a lunch if I was interested in an open, non-judgmental, agenda-free dialogue about what I was doing professionally.

I'm quite certain I was Googling his name as the ball dropped in Times Square. Much of the rest of my night was spent discussing the encounter with my wife and whether or not my skeptical nature would take him up on his offer to meet. I recall her advice as being, *"What do you have to lose? An hour of your time? Based on your intense Google research it appears that there might be much to gain."*

About a week later I reached out to the gentleman, Jay Nisberg, one of the co-authors of the book you are about to read. We set a date to meet for lunch, and my wife was right. As time would prove, there was nothing to lose and much has been gained.

Some five-years later, Jay has become a great friend and has had a clear and quantifiable impact on our business along with the contributions of his co-authors Sandy Manson and Gary Shamis. After going through the Stratagem process twice and experiencing the results first hand, we at the Sterling Organization are now firmly committed to Stratagem. Going forward, we will participate in annual off-site Stratagem sessions and have integrated it into our regular operating routine.

Having had the opportunity to preview a draft of this book, I sincerely believe that its contents and the Stratagem process are relevant to anyone with personal and/or professional goals. Stratagem will help you turn your vision into reality. It provides a clear process to facilitate the execution of your vision. The focus is not only on achieving your business goals but your personal goals as well. After all, your business is personal. This book outlines the dynamic, non-threatening process of Stratagem, which helps you and your team think outside the box while staying focused on your goals and ensuring accountability and follow up. Stratagem gets you working on the business instead of only in the business. There is no doubt that our team's participation in the Stratagem Process has produced a stronger, more cohesive and engaged team with a common vision capable of producing at a much higher level than pre-Stratagem.

I felt honored and compelled to write this forward when asked. I feel that I personally owe Jay, Gary, Sandy and Stratagem a lot. While not exclusively responsible for our company's progress and the realization of both our goals and ever-expanding vision, Stratagem has made a significant impact and I am certain our firm's ability to double our revenues, triple our profits and increase our margins by 36 percent since our first Stratagem session three-years ago, is in large part the result of participating in such.

I am forever grateful to Jay, Gary and Sandy and feel incredibly lucky to have had that chance New Year's Eve encounter with Jay. You now have their book in your hands and need not rely on luck. Enjoy and remember you have nothing to lose and much to gain.

Brian D. Kosoy
President & Chief Executive Officer
Sterling Organization

Chapter 1

Stratagem:
A Different Approach to Strategic Planning

Strategic planning efforts too often follow the same fate as New Year's resolutions. Prepared to start a fresh chapter, leaders plow full-steam into list making and goal-setting. They've got big ideas and they're putting them on paper. Plus, everyone's on board — there's a contagious energy. So, naturally, the execution starts strong. All too often that initial drive to see the plan through takes a detour, and then makes a few pit stops as daily *fires* call for attention and resources.

The strategic plan gets pushed aside, shelved and eventually buried. It collects dust. And it becomes completely irrelevant. The strategic plan created is really nothing more than a document, a wish list that gets recreated on an annual (or less often) basis when the team gathers to talk vision and set goals. If this sounds familiar, perhaps you're seeking a better way to get your vision to reality.

Stratagem is a different approach to thinking about your business today and in the future. It provides leaders with an executable vision and a clear process to get there so they can succeed. It critically bridges the business and personal goals of owners and executives.

With Stratagem, the strategic plan is a living, constantly evolving business tool. It addresses the big questions: What do I want to do with my life, and what do I want to do with my business? It offers tools to identify barriers and build steps — workable solutions — so you can reach business and personal goals. Essentially, Stratagem helps leaders create a truly executable vision for themselves and their businesses by breaking down key components of the strategic plan into tasks that can be delegated, assigned and accounted for.

Stratagem is not about creating a *strategic planning document*. It's an all-embracing, dynamic process and not a rigid form. In fact, the Stratagem process fosters productivity and creativity. It encourages leaders to think outside the box while staying focused on their vision and goals for both themselves and the business.

The crux of the process is a marriage of personal and business goals, with accountability and follow-up built into the process, which ensures that the plan is a *living document*. If done properly, it is regularly revisited and evolves with the times. Does this sound like a plan your business and life needs?

MERGING LIFE AND BUSINESS

Stop for a moment to consider, what do you want to do with your life? What do you want to do with your business? How will your business enable you to reach your life goals, achieve a standard of living, buy that vacation home, retire at a certain age or provide a legacy for the generations after you?

When the time comes to exit the business, will its harvest fulfill your personal appetite — for whatever? Many times, the answer is no. The problem with many strategic-planning processes is that they leave out a critical component: your life.

Business is personal. The two lives must intersect, and the goals set for the business must help satisfy personal goals. Otherwise, what's the point of all the hard work?

The Stratagem process will take you from vision to reality in steps, and help you build a road that secures the growth of your business and the realization of your personal goals. It's a practical method of strategic planning because it takes into account leaders' whole lives, not just isolated business components.

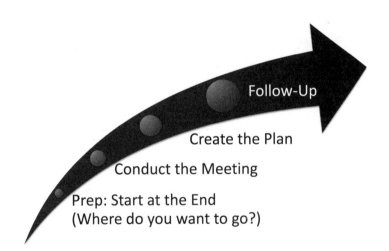

Follow-Up

Create the Plan

Conduct the Meeting

Prep: Start at the End
(Where do you want to go?)

HATCHING A 'REAL' PLAN

Stratagem was developed at Johnston Carmichael, Scotland's largest independent firm of Chartered Accountants at the start of the new millennium. The firm deals with many family and owner-managed businesses and as a result increasingly found itself engaged with their clients in those critical, too often avoided, life-changing conversations about longer-term plans for both their businesses and themselves. Johnston Carmichael's leadership identified the need to formalize and design a process to assist their clients in making these key decisions in a non-threatening and structured way.

One of the individuals who played a key role in the architecture of the process, Sandy Manson, regularly asked clients, many of whom were CEOs, to articulate their personal drivers and ambitions. Manson, now CEO of Johnston Carmichael, asked clients: *"What is it that you really want out of this life?"* Manson and his colleagues in the firm found themselves in close relationships with their clients and as such they were sufficiently trusted to have deep and critical conversations with their clients.

Manson wasn't asking solely about their business goals; he also wanted to consider personal goals — what they individually hoped to achieve. Their answers varied. Some had a target retirement age in mind. Others saw dollar signs and wanted to reach a certain financial goal. Others wanted to travel, to start new businesses, to move closer to grandchildren or to spend more time on their hobbies.

The problem was, many of these owners were not positioned in their businesses to reach these personal goals and typically spent too much time working in the business and not on the business. Their business goals failed to address personal goals — they existed in a vacuum. As a result, business owners and senior executives were often unhappy because their businesses weren't helping them get to that place in their lives that they dreamed about. They were working the business, but it wasn't working for them.

Johnston Carmichael's answer: bridge the personal and business goals. Help leaders articulate their personal aspirations and identify the business drivers that can help them reach those goals in a non-threatening environment where the participants are open and relaxed about addressing life's big decisions for themselves and their businesses. Ultimately, the team at Johnston Carmichael created a connection — and that connection is Stratagem.

The Stratagem Way

Stratagem takes business owners and leaders to a sweet spot in planning, where business and personal goals converge. It's a plan grounded in reality: This is where we are today. This is where we need to go. Built-in actionable steps and accountability tools ensure there is momentum in the plan — and that's where so many plans putter out and fail.

During the Stratagem process, participants address some of the most difficult issues for them personally and professionally. Business owners and leaders are encouraged to confront brutal facts. Let's face it, digging into the personal stuff isn't all that easy to do. But it's critical if participants are serious about reaching their goals. With Stratagem, this discussion happens in a safe, non-threatening environment.

Ultimately, Stratagem helps business owners and leaders form a habit of addressing those tough issues. It also helps them to delegate tasks so goals can be met. It aligns the team towards a common vision and set of goals — and critically it helps flush out those who are not aligned and more likely to be a handbrake on the plans for the business.

The Stratagem process leaves companies with a document that addresses issues, proposes solutions, outlines steps for reaching goals, identifies who will do what and when, and how follow-up will occur.

This 360-degree approach embeds ownership and accountability in an organization. It builds stronger, more cohesive and more energized teams. And it helps leaders realize those business and personal goals. Stratagem isn't a theory and it's very roots are embedded in a practical approach to working with business owners and leaders which has been proven over many years to work time and time again.

Ready to get started?

Chapter 2

Why Stratagem?

D o you feel like your business is running on a treadmill? You keep going and going but the direction sometimes seems unclear. Or, perhaps you've hit a rut — an obstacle is preventing the organization from moving forward. Most every business leader can say that economic factors have presented significant challenges that require a retooling of the organization to secure the sustainability of the business. How has the company emerged? Is what's in place still working?

Maybe you have realized that your personal and professional goals are not in sync — that the business is not fulfilling your personal aspirations. Issues within the business may be hindering your ability to meet goals that you set for the organization and your personal life. Is the business helping you get what you want?

Sometimes, an owner needs to simply take the pulse of the business — checkout of the day-to-day and check-in to planning mode. It's the old adage of working on the business and not working in it. And let's be honest, stepping back to honestly address issues that could be inhibiting the business from helping you achieve professional and personal goals — well, that's messy stuff that can potentially require going to uncomfortable places with your emotions and relationships. So we typically put it off, parking the issues in the *too difficult to do* tray, which is easy to do since the demands of running a business are so great that carving the time for thoughtful strategic planning seems near impossible.

Taking that dedicated time-out is essential for the business to be a success. How you spend that time is critical. Stratagem helps leaders work efficiently and effectively through business issues, harvest solutions and begin implementing them to reach goals. The planning sessions can be customized to suit any size business, and we'll show you how to do that in this book. Stratagem is a process for strategic planning, with flexibility built into this model to allow individuals and businesses to become focused, aligned and energized with the planning process rather than feeling suffocated by a long set of impersonal procedures when addressing those important and tough personal and business issues.

Stratagem enables business owners and leaders to ask:

- What are the issues for me and the business?
- How can they be addressed and resolved in a practical and feasible way?
- Who will take ownership to implement the solution — and what resources and help do they need?

Stratagem documents issues, proposes solutions and builds in accountability and ownership for the solution. So now that you know what Stratagem is and does, you may be wondering, how will my business and I benefit?

Is STRATAGEM A FIT?

Stratagem can work for your business whether you operate a generations-old, mom-and-pop shop or a global, publicly traded corporation. The process can be applied to businesses of all sizes and structures. No business is too big, too small, too simple or too complex. If you are a sole proprietor, Stratagem can work for you. And if you employ thousands, the system works as effectively.

How is this possible? Stratagem is flexible because the methodology is defined by its core principles, which don't change with the size or complexity of a business.

We know from our years of consulting experience in the United Kingdom and the United States that businesses are a lot like people. Organizations are living, breathing, changing entities with growing pains, good days and bad days. No two businesses are the same. So when we were developing Stratagem, it was critical to create a strategic-planning process that could be easily adapted and shaped to suit the needs of any business. Stratagem's flexibility will not compromise its powerful results. It can be customized and successfully implemented in any business. We're going to show you how to do that in the coming chapters.

Now, you're probably wondering: What's the catch? How much is this going to cost? Actually, you don't need a big-business budget to implement Stratagem. While bringing in an outside facilitator for planning sessions can be tremendously beneficial, Stratagem's rules-for-the-road give in-house leaders the direction to guide effective planning sessions and garner results.

So the simple answer to your question, *"Can Stratagem work for me and my business?"* is *"Yes!"* But for it to work, you must be prepared to be open, honest and willing to confront those big issues facing you and your business.

Now a question for you: Unless you have 100 percent clarity on the major issues facing you and the business, what are you waiting for?

STRATAGEM: A PLANNING LIFESTYLE

Do you feel like you've tried everything to change the way you think about the business? You've gone through a pile of books, attended conferences and lectures, even brought consultants in to help. You're convinced it's all the same story; you've been there, tried that.

Stratagem changes the way you've always done strategic planning. That's because it's a practical, 360-degree approach where you are setting goals, meeting them and then setting new ones. It becomes a mind-set and the work gets done. The ideas you hatch during a planning meeting become reality. The people who work for you are not only drinking the punch, they're lining up for seconds — because the Stratagem process is cyclical, ongoing. It's not a planning day or week. It's a planning lifestyle.

Stratagem combines today's best book-approach to identifying the future direction for you and your business, based on our review of the literature, and our years of experience helping business leaders and organizations establish strategy. What we're saying is, we've been there, read that, too. And we felt a little empty after trying other processes. Our clients wanted and needed more to succeed. Across the board the personal aspect of planning was missing — the bridge we discussed that connects individuals' aspirations with their business goals.

That's what differentiates Stratagem and is why it works for all businesses. Already, organizations in the United Kingdom and United States have benefitted from this approach, and you'll read some of their stories in the case studies throughout this book. These true, road stories are testament to Stratagem's success. By implementing the Stratagem philosophy of driving business goals to dovetail with business owners' and leaders' personal ambitions, businesses have transformed the way they operate. The resulting focus and energy Stratagem has created for them has been nothing short of remarkable.

Remember, no two organizations are the same but what they all have in common is that they are run by individuals with personal lives and goals. At the end of the day, for a business to truly be a success, it should help leaders realize their dreams.

Stratagem can work for all types of businesses because of this — it's a holistic approach to strategic planning. And that's why we say that the process evolves into a sort of planning lifestyle for leaders. It's not plan one day, create a follow-up document and then be done with it. Stratagem is a fresh way of thinking about what's next. And, as we've seen, this can be incredibly energizing for everyone involved.

Let's take a look at one of the businesses utilizing the Stratagem process before we dig into the process's details.

Case Study: Macduff Shellfish

Scotland's Macduff Shellfish was in the process of transitioning the century-old family business to the next generation. The business is nearly 130 years old, and is operated by the Beaton brothers, the third generation running the business. Over the years, Macduff Shellfish weathered its share of challenges: access to raw materials and supplies, capital shortfalls and inadequate production facilities. The constantly fluctuating market conditions were always a concern. Still, the business was profitable and had been for decades. The question was: What direction should the Beaton brothers take their family business? The brothers were at a crossroads, really digging for what was next. That's when Stratagem came into play.

The Beaton brothers had heard about Stratagem and decided they would try it for themselves and their business and see if the process would assist them to build a better business and to create alignment and clarity about their own personal longer-term plans. Quickly following their first Stratagem session in February 2003, the Beaton brothers made some big decisions. They agreed to expand their business into continental Europe and to grow their production facilities. The Beatons worked their plan and began making significant headway. They revisited their plan and scheduled periodic Stratagem sessions as needed. These follow-up sessions updated and reaffirmed their direction.

During the sessions, the Beatons analyzed their business' strengths and weaknesses, and discussed their personal passions for the business — how each brother excelled in the organization and how the business could best benefit from their individual talents. They then began to align the business and its structure with their personal strengths and aspirations. Stratagem gave them time to pause and articulate why they were putting such enormous energy into their business. They were making serious demands of themselves and their families — they needed to define the purpose for the sacrifices and identify the rewards for working so hard. These discussions helped the brothers emerge with a common vision, renewed energy for the business and a solid, evolving plan for taking the business in that new direction.

Macduff Shellfish defined its main product lines — langoustines, crabs, scallops and whelk. They innovated ways to offer fishermen the best prices and market security, which is a critical need for fisherman. The brothers built a processing facility with greater capacity and then expanded their customer base quickly to utilize that capacity. Today, Macduff Shellfish is Europe's largest shellfish company. While it was the Beaton brothers who delivered the results with their team, they don't underestimate the value Stratagem delivered in assisting them to grow the business from $16.1 million in 2002 sales revenues to 2012 sales revenues in excess of $57 million. The profitability of the business grew handsomely, too, and the brothers were able to all align themselves behind a clear strategy for them and the business, which included bringing in a new investor in 2011.

Stratagem didn't do the work. It didn't create the Beaton brothers' success. What Stratagem did was provide a forum where the brothers could strategize and a framework for them to build their success. It became a way of leading the business for the Beatons, who continue to regularly revisit their strategic plans and set new goals for their business. Stratagem became a mind-set.

Chapter 3

Implementing Stratagem

The Stratagem process is an ongoing affair — you launch it during a day (or two) away from the business but the work doesn't stop when the meeting is over. During that planning time, a mind-set shift occurs. You begin to think differently about your life and the business, and how the goals you set coexist in these worlds. Your attitude about strategic planning will change as you focus on the big picture and link those personal and business objectives. You'll learn ways to spend your energy and resources on activities that will help you reach those goals. And when you leave the session, you, like so many of the business owners and leaders who have successfully implemented Stratagem, will feel re-energized, reinvigorated and refocused on where you are today and where you're headed in business and life.

Implementation of Stratagem involves four major steps:
1. *Preparation: Start at the End* — Set the stage for a successful meeting. Critical in this process, is deciding who should actually attend the first session.
2. *Conduct the Meeting* — Lay down some ground rules and clarify if there are any taboo topics. Remember the process must create a non-threatening environment. It is best to have someone from outside the business who is trusted to facilitate the session.

3. *Creation of the Plan* — Agree with both the personal and business vision and goals; identify the respective issues and solutions (a hard copy of the strategic plan is produced as a result of the meeting).
4. *Follow-up Activity* — Accountability measures and target dates for achieving the agreed action points, as well as setting dates for follow-up reviews on progress.

Preparation — Start at the End

Stratagem pushes you to begin planning for the session by focusing on the end-goals first. What results should the meeting yield? What do you hope to accomplish? From there, you, the facilitator and your colleagues work together from that endpoint to where you are today. What will it take to get where you want to be in business and life?

So job No. 1 is to decide who should attend the Stratagem session and then ensuring that everyone attending understands what it will entail and that they need to be prepared to be open and honest, which may involve confronting some brutal facts and difficult issues. The better the planning and expectations are for what you wish the Stratagem session will accomplish, the more productive and creative the session will be. There are long-term goals, and there are mini-goals, if you will — steps along the way that help you reach that vision. Stratagem helps you obtain that gold medal at the end of the race: the big goal. The most common goal for a Stratagem session is to help give the business owners and leaders complete clarity and alignment around their own personal and business goals. Equally, because Stratagem is so flexible, you can set more specific goals such as focusing on determining more revenue-generating activities for your business (with the big goal in mind); or repositioning the business to be more competitive in a changing market (with the big goal in mind); or to pass the business on to the next generation (again, with that big goal in mind). There can be no guarantee about what will be the outcome once the door to the planning session is opened, only that the process has been proven over many years of practical application to work time and time again.

Be prepared for the discussion about these ideas to take you to unpredicted, but rewarding places.

Conduct the Meeting

Stratagem works because planning sessions evolve into a creative brain dump with parameters. The discussion stays focused on goals because participants understand in advance how the meeting will be conducted. Usually with a trusted facilitator to guide them through the process, the group navigates sensitive territory. Tough issues are managed in spite of any tension, and productive resolutions are outlined. Stratagem helps preserve relationships as thorny subjects are discussed in a safe, non-threatening environment. But in order for this environment to exist, you must set expectations for all participants in advance.

We recommend sharing an outline of how Stratagem works with participants in advance. Use the framework on pages 31–33. This simple framework will give participants a clear picture of how they will be expected to contribute to the planning session. They can get into the Stratagem mind-set before the meeting is called to order. In practice there is usually no shortage of constructive contribution from the participants because they feel so passionate about the subjects at hand — the plans for themselves and the business.

Creation of The Plan

The tangible result of a Stratagem session is a hard copy of a strategic plan with a section setting out individual participant's personal goals. This living document is a strong business tool and discipline that will guide your organization on the road to reaching those business and personal goals. It's a road map — and there are checkpoints along the way. The plan is a starting point, and you'll revise this as you continue applying the Stratagem process. The plan captures the conclusions from the discussion that took place during the Stratagem session, confirms the action items and goals, and gives participants a clear vision for themselves and the business as well as setting out the key priorities to focus on.

Follow-Up Activity

With the solid preparation for the session, and the effective planning that took place during the meeting, you are now ready to implement the plan. You're not alone in this task — you can continue to check in with your facilitator and advisers We recommend that to get the best results from Stratagem you engage the people in your organization every step of the way, because they are the ones who will expedite the plan. Based on decisions made during the Stratagem session, you'll assign roles and goals to key players in your organization, and you'll hold each member of your team accountable. Forget the old way of unilateral decision-making. In today's complex business environment, we believe sustainable results come from empowering and engaging your team behind a clearly articulated strategy. The results from aligning everyone behind a common plan are very powerful.

The Stratagem Workbook

So far, we've given you the broad framework of how Stratagem is implemented. From here, this book will walk you through the process in detail so you can launch Stratagem at your company with, or without, the help of an outside facilitator. (We'll discuss the advantages of bringing in a trusted facilitator in the next chapter.) You may feel that undertaking a Stratagem session is somewhat daunting or feel anxious about letting go when discussing important personal and business issues. Or you may not be quite sure how Stratagem works in practice, but when broken down into practical, workable steps, you'll see that Stratagem is a natural way of walking through the wants and needs of your personal and professional lives, and ensuring that those two circles intersect. And, as we have stated, Stratagem is a 360-degree approach — so the planning and implementation keeps going on when you have reached a goal. You set a new one and start working again. This sustains momentum; it keeps organizations fresh, creative, competitive and profitable. Stratagem becomes an energizing and challenging mind-set that has brought very significant benefits to many individuals and organizations since its creation more than a decade ago. You will find the full, usable workbook in Appendix II.

A number of the chapters that follow offer a series of workbook exercises to help you dig deeper as you work through the Stratagem process. The chapters guide you through the main activities that make up the Stratagem process:

- **Preparation:** First, you'll set the stage for a successful Stratagem session by deciding who attends, who facilitates, what the rules are, what you can and cannot discuss (although in our experience there is very little, if anything, which is not discussed). You will also agree on a suitable get-away-from-it-all venue for the Stratagem session.

- **The Stratagem Meeting**

  — *Setting the Vision and Aligning Life and Business Goals*: Then, you'll discuss and share personal goals, set the vision for the business and share business goals, working through exercises to help shape a purposeful direction for you and your organization. This will consider the vision for you and the business as well as identify the main strategic goals around which the business owners and leaders can align themselves.

  — *Business Review*: Now you will get into more detail by taking stock of the main strengths, weaknesses, opportunities and threats in each key function of your business, from marketing and sales to operations and finance. In this way you will give each of the building blocks of your business a good shake and identify what works well and what needs to be improved. This will usually include understanding the competitive landscape you are operating in and identify other products and services that might deliver additional value to your business.

- **Building the Plan:** The actual strategic plan resulting from the Stratagem session will include action points and responsibilities — it's a living document that you'll revisit as goals are met, and revise as you hold further sessions and set new goals. All participants should and usually do take ownership for delivering the strategy and action points set out in the plan arising from the session.

- **The Stratagem Habit:** Stratagem is a mind-set and a business way of life. We'll discuss how to follow up on goals to make sure that real, actionable results are coming to fruition. We'll also explain how you can engage the people in your business in the plan.

With this framework in mind, you are now ready to begin preparation for holding your own Stratagem session, see Chapter 4.

Barriers to Strategic Planning

What prevents business owners and leaders from attaining their business and personal goals? And why do so many strategic plans created with great intentions end up collecting dust? Because preparing, creating and implementing a plan takes a real commitment — and it's a process that involves those three steps, plus constant follow-up and accountability.

In our experience, here are the main reasons why so many strategic plans fail. Have any of the following obstacles prevented plans from being successfully implemented at your organization?
- A firm's culture means alignment and change is difficult to achieve.
- It's difficult to find time to stand back from the frontline and think bigger picture.
- Self-serving interests and agendas.
- Lack of understanding of what's involved in strategic planning.
- Reluctance of leaders to let go.
- *"I always thought we should do this but never quite knew how to go about it."*
- Anxiety as to what might be the consequences of a strategic planning process.
- Too much focus on short-term results.

Sterling Case 1: Stratagem Discovery

Shortly after Johnston Carmichael had designed and launched Stratagem in 2002, Jay Nisberg, a well-known adviser to the accounting profession across the globe, had been working with the firm in Scotland and immediately recognized the potential and power of the process. Over the years since that point, Nisberg kept in touch with Sandy Manson, CEO of Johnston Carmichael, on the continuing success of the application of Stratagem in the United Kingdom and encouraged him to promote Stratagem to a much wider international market.

A suitable opportunity for Stratagem was identified by Nisberg in 2010 with entrepreneur Brian Kosoy and his business, the Sterling Organization. Sterling is a vertically oriented, private equity, real estate investment firm based in Palm Beach, Fla., with offices throughout Florida, North Carolina, Texas and Chicago. In 2010, the firm participated in Stratagem under the guidance of Nisberg and Manson. *"I had known Jay for some time, and he had always shown an interest in our relatively young but rapidly growing business,"* says Kosoy, a partner at the firm. *"I felt we had little to lose and much to gain."*

The culture at Sterling is, *"Be the best at all we do,"* Kosoy says. *"No detail of our business is too small to not produce the absolute best product possible. Because I trusted Jay personally and admired his reputation in the industry, we were eager to try anything that could make our business and team better, and potentially improve the value and quality of the product we deliver to clients, investors and partners."*

For a firm to grow and thrive there needs to be more than a small group of individuals driving it forward, Kosoy says. The long-term idea at Sterling is to institutionalize a culture of success so clients invest in the firm rather than an individual. This evolution does not happen overnight. Kosoy says his firm has a long way to go, but Stratagem made it clear that the team needed to begin executing on this mission now.

Why Stratagem? *"We felt it made a lot of sense to get the whole team out of the trenches and into the situation room for a couple of days to take stock and lift our heads up to view the horizon,"* Kosoy says. *"The Stratagem sessions had such a positive impact on our business and team."*

Here, Kosoy shares how the Stratagem process unfolded at Sterling and the key takeaways the group gained from the sessions.

Leverage talent: Through Stratagem, Kosoy says it was clear the firm was not leveraging the talent of key members consistently. Some team members were working on time-consuming matters that did not maximize their talents or output, tasks that could be accomplished by other employees in a more cost-effective, efficient manner.

Pass the hat: *"Because we want everything we do to be as perfect as possible, senior management was reticent to let go of tasks that could be accomplished by other team members in the organization,"* Kosoy says. In order to move forward, these senior members had to, *"get out of the weeds."* Their focus on details that others could handle was stunting growth and causing the team to potentially miss opportunities. But this was not obvious until Stratagem.

"Because we were growing at a healthy clip and performing well in a very tough market, we really didn't notice the issue," Kosoy says. *"Once the Stratagem process brought it to light, we realized we could have been pushing our talented team to use deeper levels of their talents more consistently, which would have led us to be more efficient in our growth trajectory."*

Learning to let go and give up control is not an easy thing to do. *"But it's necessary when your business transitions from a small, entrepreneurial shop to something marginally bigger,"* Kosoy says.

Defining roles: *"It became clear it was time to opportunistically deepen our team's bench strength,"* Kosoy says. No longer could senior members be involved in numerous facets of the business. Clearly defined roles and responsibilities were necessary. This way, senior members could focus on those activities that propel the business forward, while dedicating tasks that could be performed more efficiently to other colleagues.

Identifying fears: Stratagem uncovered some common fears shared among senior management at Sterling. The firm's most significant, collective fear was that *"something, anything could fall through the cracks,"* Kosoy says. The team was worried about a systems failure. This traced back to the importance of clearly defining each person's role in the organization and ensuring there was no overlap and no gaps.

"Stratagem highlighted that the fear of failure is clearly one of the driving forces and common characteristics behind each member of our senior management team," Kosoy

sums up. *"As a result, we came away feeling we needed to opportunistically improve our team and hire individuals whose relationships and core competencies complemented but were different than the team we had in place. That way, we could fill the gaps and leverage a deeper team."*

Chapter 4

Preparation:
Setting the Stage for Stratagem

Now, we begin to answer some basic pre-planning questions to ensure a successful Stratagem session. Who should be involved? Who should facilitate? What topics do you want to address? When will you hold the meeting, and for how long? Where should the meeting take place — off-site? Which issues do you feel Stratagem will help resolve (this gets into some initial goal setting)? How will you prepare participants for the Stratagem process?

This chapter helps you answer these questions so you can properly prepare for a Stratagem session and optimize the time you spend laying the groundwork for a living strategic plan — a dynamic road map that will guide you toward personal and professional aspirations. You'll decide which members of your team will be valuable architects in your Stratagem session and in creating the resulting plan. You'll set some rules for the session to ensure open, honest communication, respect for all opinions and an outcome of stronger relationships among leaders. As you build your plan, you're fortifying your team — and this is critical, because lack of unity and alignment among the leadership of the business is one reason why strategic plans can and do fail.

Now, let's get to work setting the stage for Stratagem.

SET THE OBJECTIVES

What are your objectives for the Stratagem session? What is the purpose? Do you intend to develop a strategic plan for the whole business, an element of the business, or a specific department such as marketing, sales or research and development? Nail down what you want to achieve with Stratagem. What's hurting in your business? What could be improved in your business? Is everyone clear about the future direction of the business and what their specific role is in achieving success for the business?

Once you define the purpose of the Stratagem meeting, you'll enter the session with a clear idea of who should attend and ensure that attendees are put at ease about what's on the agenda for Stratagem. Our experience has shown that the first Stratagem sessions have often been held with the specific remit of setting or refining the entire strategy for the owners and leaders of the business and, as such, is a broad ranging and comprehensive session that addresses the main personal and business goals and strategic priorities. Therefore, the Stratagem process described in this book uses that holistic approach as the default and you can then refine the process should you wish to address only a specific business issue with Stratagem.

Please note, however, that there can be no predetermined outcome for a Stratagem session. Once the process starts it can take you in all sorts of surprising, enlightening and rewarding directions. This is exactly why Stratagem creates so much alignment, engagement and energy for the participants.

Facilitation and Participation

Now that you have identified the purpose of your Stratagem session, you may want to include key decision-makers and executives in appropriate departments of your business.

Who attends, and who leads the meeting? This depends on the size of your organization and goals for the meeting. You may include key executives, family members or limit the meeting to a specific department, such as sales if that will be the focus of your session. The people who will be in charge of helping you implement any strategic plan should be present; as should advisers and others who you feel can bring valuable insight to the conversation. You want participants to be honest, fair and respectful.

Our experience shows that in privately owned businesses, it is usually best to always start with the business owners because unless the owners are aligned about the future of the business then there is little point in the executive team leading the business and agreeing on a strategy which the owners don't buy into! In many cases the owners are sufficiently open with their key executives and they are happy to include them in the Stratagem session or a second session is held with the key executives once the owners have clarified their own personal and business strategy.

One of the most important people you'll invite to this meeting is the facilitator. We strongly recommend that you consider using a trusted person to facilitate your Stratagem session. This person should not be an advocate for any party involved in the meeting, but rather choose a trusted and objective person who will ensure that the session is conducted in the right atmosphere, one conducive to creative thinking and open to constructive dialogue. The facilitator can be a great asset when navigating through sticky subjects if, and when, they arise. Ultimately, the facilitator will ensure that the Stratagem process described in this book is carried out and that the objectives of the session are met and documented. While Stratagem will encourage participants to be open and honest about all aspects of their own personal and business goals, the facilitator has the important task of ensuring that relationships are always kept intact and that no participant is taken to a place in the discussion they clearly don't want to go. A good facilitator will have the emotional intelligence to sense just how to deal with such situations and the session can be more productive if a particular subject is parked and revisited. However our own experience is that there are very few issues that are not satisfactorily resolved during the session because a well-planned Stratagem session creates the environment where participants feel safe to be entirely open and honest. Further, the facilitator can be a valuable player with whom the business owners and leaders can follow-up to ensure that the plan is being implemented.

The person appointed to facilitate the Stratagem session has important homework to do before the session. He or she should try and ensure they have a reasonably detailed understanding of the business, its operations, existing strategy (assuming there is one), the market it competes in and its financial performance and position. This planning work on the part of the facilitator is important so that valuable time during the Stratagem session is not wasted asking basic questions about the business and its operations. We recommend that the business owners or leaders furnish the appointed facilitator with whatever information the facilitator feels would be helpful to have in advance.

The Stratagem Environment

Stratagem sessions typically last one or two days, but no fixed timetable should be set because the nature of Stratagem is that you want no time barriers impeding the conversation Generally, though, it will be very obvious to both the facilitator and the participants when the Stratagem session is complete and has run its natural course. The participants tend to feel mentally exhausted but hugely exhilarated and energized. If you are holding a two-day session be prepared for participants' brains to be buzzing at the end of day one, which can affect sleep patterns! Experience suggests that a Stratagem session for up to four people can typically be conducted within one day but with more participants, two days tends to be appropriate.

The most effective Stratagem sessions are usually held at off-site locations so participants can fully immerse in the discussion without distractions from daily business activities. One of the Stratagem rules is that all participants switch off mobile devices during the session although email and voice mail is typically checked during the breaks. While you'll set an agenda for the meeting, Stratagem meetings should not end because time has run out. The agenda will suggest an indicative time for the session, and if there isn't enough time to cover all the key issues, the agenda or timescale should be adjusted so all the important matters can be addressed. It is always best to plan enough time because the most effective Stratagem sessions are held when there is no feeling of time constraints. The facilitator will assist with the time management of the session and the flow of the schedule — how the group moves from one item on the agenda to the next. There should never be an unnatural stop to any important discussion during Stratagem. Tabling an active or perhaps uncomfortable discussion will only result in a lack of participants' buy-in. Be prepared to be flexible in both the allocation of time and the sequence of the subjects and issues discussed.

As for location, we suggest you choose a neutral location outside of your business where participants can feel relaxed and at ease. That way, participants will be more open and will focus on the agenda when phones aren't ringing and emails aren't beeping. The venue should also be private so there are no concerns about confidentiality.

There's an energy that comes with holding a meeting outside of the office. The day is immediately established as different, important. Some locations that have proven successful include hotel or resort meeting rooms, or meeting spaces in private clubs or country retreats. All participants should be able to sit comfortably around the same table and across from each other. The room should promote complete engagement so that everyone can have honest discussions about themselves and the business. The seating plan around the table is also important to consider to get the most out of a constructive interaction.

You may decide to organize the meeting as an overnight retreat, and there are benefits to extending the stay. When day one is completed the participants are usually left on their own to continue the conversation. The topics remain fresh and they can percolate over discussions rather than riveting back into their busy lives at home, where they are forced to drop work and pick up on other duties.

A breakfast meeting the next morning is a great way to reconvene the group and to follow up on the previous day's discussions. The energy from the prior day's meeting continues, and conversation will buzz over issues they have been mulling over. The group is still immersed in the issues and problem-solving solutions. The momentum is going strong — and that's a great way to kick off a plan.

Do Participants Need to Prepare for a Stratagem Session?

The only preparation participants need to do is clear their calendars and show up with a clear head and a willingness to participate actively and openly. Our experience is that when executives at various levels in an organization are trusted and asked to participate in a Stratagem session, they do not abuse that opportunity but rather act constructively and respectfully in the interests of the business.

SETTING SOME RULES

One function of the outline and planning is setting some ground rules, and we're talking about taboo topics here. Stratagem is designed to constructively resolve long-simmering issues and to form workable plans for overcoming obstacles to reach goals. But if rules are not established, the risk is that the session takes participants to places where they are just not ready to go. Stratagem is not a gripe session; it's a focused planning session. So make those out-of-bounds topics clear in advance so everyone understands that the objective is to dig into the problems and find solutions. The facilitator is charged with sensing when the discussion is moving into territory that is not constructive and for getting the dialogue back on track.

At the same time, Stratagem sessions give participants the freedom to express their ideas and offer practical solutions to the problems presented. This can mean introducing uncomfortable topics and can cause uncomfortable conversations. This is OK. In fact, these sticky discussions are often the most revealing and productive. And that's why a facilitator is usually best involved, to help guide these discussions down a constructive, solution-producing path.

Confidentiality Is Absolutely Necessary During Stratagem Sessions

Participants must agree that what happens at Stratagem, stays there. Whatever issues are presented in that room, stay there. Ideas floated during the meeting do not become watercooler chat back at the office. Get the word of every participant that he or she understands and respects this confidentiality agreement.

TROUBLESHOOTING A STRATAGEM SESSION

Stratagem sessions can get uncomfortable for some participants, and that's OK. What's important is how sticky situations are handled — that feedback is constructive, everyone's ideas are respected, and participants actively listen and openly share. These things are not easy and can test even a cohesive team. This is where a facilitator can be especially helpful. Consider enlisting a trusted facilitator to your team so they can ensure that the Stratagem session is productive and positive.

Here are three common issues that crop up during Stratagem sessions and how to deal with them.

1. Hogging the microphone: Some people are natural participators — they like to talk out problems, and they like to be heard. They sometimes wax on and on … and on. They may interrupt others to make a point, or talk a point to exhaustion. You need to set limits and enforce them. We're not suggesting that you pull out a timer, but the facilitator will be able to ensure the appropriate airtime is given to each participant.

2. Distracted by 'sparks': The email keeps beeping on his or her smartphone. His or her texting fingers are flicking across the keypad full force. Remind everyone participating that the No. 1 priority is the meeting, not whatever fire must be put out back at the office. You're asking for undivided attention one workday out of the year. If there is a serious issue that requires immediate attention, then call for a break. That's why planning for the day is so important, so that everyone knows they must have organized themselves and their teams to survive a day or two without them. It's a good idea to arrange for cell phone/email breaks so participants can quickly check in without disrupting the flow of the Stratagem session.

3. The Glossed Over Issue: When in a group discussion such as Stratagem, which calls for sharing of thoughts and ideas, people are always listening and picking up vibes and messages that may not be particularly obvious. The facilitator has a role to listen intently and make note of those issues or messages that might be quietly given but are vital in ensuring the right answer is obtained. The facilitator should listen and ask; they should share experiences but not tell. If the facilitator identifies a potential issue, they should drill into it with the group and not just gloss it over. It may be that it's a thorny one, but by gently probing, the facilitator can determine just how far it can be constructively pushed.

SS&G Case: Financial Services

Before SS&G Financial Services began using Stratagem, it was a $10 million firm that annually set goals and conducted strategic planning exercises. But as partner Gary Shamis says, *"They were always shelf plans."* Write it, print it, bind it, shelve it — there it sits, collecting dust.

The problem with strategic planning the old way, which essentially meant gathering together key personnel to talk about big-picture ideas without putting any real accountability measures in place, is that the goals were just way too broad. *"You were trying to improve everything — and the result was you ended up improving nothing,"* Shamis says.

Since implementing Stratagem, Solon, Ohio-based SS&G has grown to a $70 million firm, and most of the growth has been organic. SS&G sets five or six initiatives at Stratagem meetings, held twice each year. In one year, the firm will accomplish about 10 initiatives. And in five years, that adds up to 50. *"If you do that versus book-shelving a strategic plan, you'll move your organization forward big time,"* Shamis says. *"And that is what happened to us at SS&G."*

Stratagem and the power of executing change through the process has given SS&G a competitive advantage over the largest firms in Ohio, and in the country. *"We went from a mid-cap firm to the second largest in the state,"* Shamis reports.

Shamis is passionate about Stratagem. He had been conducting a brand of this planning at SS&G before he met Manson, co-founder of Stratagem. Shamis and Manson were involved in starting an international alliance of CPA firms, and they became friends over the years. They began comparing notes on their methods of strategic planning, and Shamis realized that his accountability and execution-focused style matched Manson's Stratagem concept.

Today, Shamis leads Stratagem at SS&G and facilitates other organizations in implementing the process. *"Stratagem has enhanced our ability to identify challenges and opportunities, and move forward,"* Shamis says. *"It has given us the ability to execute progress."*

Specifically, here is how Stratagem helped SS&G accelerate growth and elevate its position as a leading CPA firm:

Choosing participants: SS&G involves its seven partners in the Stratagem process, along with its four advisory board members. This 11-person executive group represents the whole firm and the goals of all owners, which include three cultural aspects: growth, being employee-centric and client service. If SS&G involved every *owner* in the business, because of the way the firm is structured, that would mean including 40-plus individuals in the Stratagem session. It's better for SS&G to keep Stratagem meetings limited to the highest-level executives so the firm can efficiently work through the process.

Identifying strategic initiatives: SS&G stays away from the nitty-gritty and reserves Stratagem for significant items that will advance the firm. These items always relate back to SS&G's business goals (growth, employee-centric, client service). During the Stratagem meeting, a list of strategic initiatives is generated, and no limits are set. One example is SS&G's initiative to retool its existing private equity effort. *"Next, what we do is add meat to the bone,"* Shamis says of filling out the tasks related to this initiative. Those include packaging, collateral and other branding efforts. *"We'll develop some of the implementation plan and assign the execution."* An individual in the organization becomes responsible for overseeing the success of this initiative — and that might be an executive staff member or someone involved elsewhere in the organization.

Measuring progress: Twice each year, the partners and advisory board meet to review Stratagem initiatives and progress, and to set new initiatives. *"Stratagem is a way to take those initiatives and spread the responsibility upon the whole firm, so you end up leveraging this important quality of execution,"* Shamis says. Execution and accountability are two aspects of Stratagem that set it apart from other types of strategic planning. And as we have discussed throughout the book, the crux of what makes Stratagem different is the way it addresses personal and business goals.

Keeping the momentum: *"Business today is about reaction and speed,"* Shamis says. Conducting semi-annual Stratagem sessions keeps SS&G on target and constantly moving forward. *"You can't guarantee success unless you execute,"* Shamis says.

Chapter 5

Getting Personal: The Stratagem Meeting — Setting the Vision and Aligning Life and Business Goals

All your preparation is done and the facilitator and participants are now in the Stratagem meeting at an out-of-office location. After the facilitator has completed the welcome and introduction, the first questions that need to be asked are:

- What do you want to achieve personally?
- What do you want the business to achieve?

These two simple questions are the crux of Stratagem. The business must feed personal goals; otherwise you're just working. Activities that take place in your business must help drive the organization toward the vision you have for the company and the vision you have for how you will live your life. When these worlds are kept separate, a business can plug along meeting big goals and even experiencing great success. But the life goals an owner or business leader wants to achieve may be completely overrun. And likewise, a business owner who uses the organization to fuel personal goals and interests will lose touch with the organization's purpose.

Today, we talk a lot about balance. How much work and life intermingle is a growing concern among business owners and their employees. More than ever before, we're examining our lifestyles and wondering how time spent achieving professional successes is enriching our whole lives. The question is, what are we really doing about achieving a balance and synergy where life and business are driving toward the same finish line?

Ideally, the vision you have for your business will help you realize the lifestyle you dream of having. If you'd like to retire at a certain age and travel the world, your role in the business should afford you the flexibility to do so while ensuring strong management of the firm while you are away. But this isn't all about retirement. It's about how you're living now, too. How does your business afford you the time to pursue life goals like travel, a hobby or more time with family?

By moving forward with a vision for your business, you can establish goals — targets that help you achieve this vision. Objectives are steps along the way that help you meet each goal. Every business activity is led with a purpose: why you're doing what you do, and how that fits into the big picture. Your people understand why tasks they are responsible for are important, and what their roles are in pursuing the big vision. This empowers leaders and their teams to work with passion, purpose and accountability.

The Vision Pyramid

Vision: The big picture.

Goals: Targets that help you achieve your vision.

Objectives: Steps along the way that help you achieve your goals and vision

I Had a Dream

Back to the key Stratagem question: What do you want to achieve, and what do you want to achieve in your business? The answer will help shape the vision for your organization. A vision gives direction and purpose to business and life and without a vision you are simply turning up and going to work every day. A vision creates energy and alignment, the synergy we talked about. A vision supports the balance you are seeking.

It's weighty stuff, creating a vision statement — what you are aiming to be. But you don't have to chain yourself to the vision you determine today. Visions change. You'll continue to revisit your vision as events in your business and personal life present challenges and opportunities.

For example, a successful businessman learns he has cancer and fast-forwards his succession plan so he can sell the business, focus on his health and enjoy the remainder of his life. His goals no longer include increasing sales by expanding into new territories. He realizes that his life and business are inextricably connected — an owner cannot divorce the two. So the vision for his business must change so the business can support his personal circumstances.

In another example, a businesswoman who had planned on passing the business along to her family recognizes that her oldest daughter, whom she hoped was going to take over, has other interests. Her daughter has changed her business/life vision, so the owner must change hers. She approaches the business with renewed drive, preparing it for an eventual sale (perhaps many years down the road). Her vision for the business changes so she can build an organization that will garner a higher price, thus giving her more to retire on later.

Or, an owner discovers a great opportunity where the business can retool to be the first to introduce a new product/service. This "aha" moment changes everything — sales goals, ideas for expansion, resources, personnel, and so on. Thus, the vision changes.

Manson recollects that one of the earliest Stratagem sessions he facilitated involved a business owned by a husband and wife. Before they had even discussed the vision for the business, the main issue that was flushed out during the discussion on personal goals was that the wife was very worried about her husband's health and the fact that he was rarely at home because of the demands of the business. This key issue shaped much of the subsequent Stratagem discussion, where a resolution was found.

Now, think about the vision for your business and life. Step back and dream a little. Where do you see yourself sitting at 8 a.m. on a Monday five years from now? Ten years from now? What does your list of accomplishments look like at that point? What have you gained personally and professionally? Now, you can craft a vision that will make these dreams a reality.

MAKE THE VISION CONTAGIOUS

Now that you have a vision, you must pass it on to the people who work at your company. Help them catch the bug. Many people in your organization may be happy to simply do their job. But when you attach a vision to their tasks, they begin to see how they play a role in the big picture. They better understand how those tasks really matter to the success of the company. Manson tells of one Stratagem session where the business owner went into the company workshop the day after the session and got all his staff together and shared with them for the first time the vision he had for the business. The owner said it was such an exhilarating experience to share this with his people and they shared his excitement about the potential for the business.

Question: Are you leading or just doing a job? How are you spreading the vision for your company to the people who work for you? Do they understand the big picture — and do you?

GET TO THE CORE

A company's vision can change and the goals it sets also will change. But the core values of the organization should remain strong and steady. Core values set the tone and culture of your business — they determine what behavior is acceptable in your business and what behavior is not. It's the personality aspect of your organization. Who are you? How do your people act and behave? What makes you different from competitors? Why do clients like you? What do you want people — vendors, clients, competitors — to say about you?

Core values define the way your business will behave as you set and reach goals, and work toward realizing your vision. They're the rules of conduct. They are guidelines for how people in your organization should act and how they should approach their jobs.

For example, one company's core value is, *"We put clients first."* No matter what, clients are the priority. If employees have to stay at work after hours to complete a project for a client, they will do so. Another organization's core value is to, *"Focus on long-term value rather than short-term profit."* This core value shapes the decisions managers make on a daily basis. They'll ask themselves, is this opportunity good for us in the long run?

Core values help define who you want to hire, who you want to do business with, how you'll gain an edge over the competition, and essentially what you want everyone to know about your company.

Here are some common core values:
- Treating people fairly.
- Conducting business in an ethical, transparent manner.
- Providing ongoing employee training opportunities.
- Respecting individuals.
- Encouraging creativity.
- Empowering employees to bring new ideas to the organization.
- Establishing a diverse workforce.
- Selling or creating the highest-quality products possible.
- Giving back to the community.
- Focusing on sustainability.
- Creating value for shareholders.

Core values can be less specific. For example, *patience* — a company will take the time to do the work and do it right. People in the organization are held to this standard. Or *creativity* — the company values new ideas and fosters an environment where employees at all levels can contribute.

Stratagem will help you define the core values of the business, but this is work you should begin doing prior to the session. While you will not typically spend a great deal of time flushing out core values during a Stratagem session, it's important to define core values so you can link those to the goals you will achieve and the vision you establish for business and life. All these puzzle pieces fit together to form a solid, valuable strategic plan for your organization. Critical with core values is their authenticity, that everyone who works in your business sees them as genuine and that the owners and the leaders of the business live by them and don't merely pay lip service to them. That's why we believe one of the key steps following a discussion during Stratagem to determine core values is to consult your staff about whether they agree with the core values you identify. This process creates a lot of buy-in throughout the organization.

Accountability Is the Key to Implementing Core Values

It's one thing to know what you believe and set ground rules so your people understand how to act. It's another thing to live those rules and create an environment that supports those core values. The most successful organizations have a culture and processes that ensure their core values are constantly reinforced.

Workbook Exercise: Understanding Your Personal and Business Goals?

As we've stated, this is a process that requires some personal insight and honest self-examination for you to receive its full benefits. Here is a brief look at the exercises the process will take you through. The complete workbook is in Appendix II.

By answering these high-level questions about your personal and business life, and openly sharing them with the rest of the participants, you'll begin to shape the framework for a set of goals where these two circles intersect.

PERSONAL GOALS:

- What motivated you to get into business?

- The thing you most enjoy about your current role is ...

- Are you happy with your current role?

- If you had a magic wand, what would you change about your current role?

- The balance between work and home is:
  - ☐ About right
  - ☐ Work too hard
  - ☐ Could take on more challenging work

- How successful do you feel? (0 = low, 10 = high)
  Score _____

- What keeps you awake at night?

- What are your plans and thoughts on an eventual exit from or succession in the business?

- At what age would you like to retire?

- Do you regularly review your own personal financial plans?

- Additional comments:

BUSINESS GOALS:
- Where do you want the business to be in five years?

- What are the priorities for the business?

- If you had a magic wand, what would you change that would have the biggest positive impact on your business?

- What are your thoughts on the current level of bank borrowing?

- How dependent is the business on you?
    - ☐ Not at all
    - ☐ Fairly
    - ☐ Totally

- Do you have succession plans in place for transfer of ownership?

- Do you have succession plans in place for key positions?

- How motivated do you think the company's employees are? (0 = low, 10 = high)

  Current _____   Target _____

- Do you have a structured sales and marketing plan?

- What changes would you make to your sales and marketing activities?

- How should you measure the success of your business?

- Which factors, if any, are holding you back from reaching your business goals?

- What changes do you see in your industry?

- What is the potential for new products and services?

- Additional comments:

Sterling Case 2: The Chairlift Theory

Kosoy shares how his firm, the Sterling Organization, used Stratagem to build a stronger team and position his company for growth and success in the following lessons learned:

The Chairlift Theory

Recruiting talent to balance the skills of existing senior management became a key focus at Sterling. Kosoy explains his Chairlift Theory here and why this action step, realized during the Stratagem session, was so important.

In the Chairlift Theory of life and business, if you and your team keep riding a chairlift with the same folks at the same ski resort, only so many opportunities can present themselves. Your view of the world becomes quite insular and limited. It's hard to get a broad market view, even from the top of a mountain because you are always looking from the same vantage point. Additionally, it's almost impossible to see the institutional fault lines within your organization.

If you add team members who have ridden different chairlifts at different mountain resorts and have taken in the world from different peaks, you will have a broader view as an institution. You'll gain fresh perspective so you can see those fault lines and bring fresh ideas so you can strengthen weaknesses. Also, these new team members can bring more relationships to leverage because they know different folks who have been skiing at the other mountain resort where your firm doesn't have a relationship.

Our business, plain and simple, is very much a relationships business. The ability to accelerate relationships through a new team member is significant. The people we bring on board can provide exponential opportunities and help us build beyond what we could internally. Simply put, we need to look outside our organization to find serious growth.

You, too, will try new resorts with your new team members as they introduce you to their network. You never know who you might sit next to on that new chairlift. In fact, my partner and the origin of our relationship can be traced back to a chairlift ride.

Chapter 6

The Business Review: The Stratagem Meeting — Shaking the Building Blocks of the Business

Now that you have discussed your personal goals, set the vision for the business and set business goals, it's time to look inside your organization in detail. In this section of the Stratagem meeting, you'll dissect the working parts of your business, from sales and marketing to production. Think of these exercises as components of an annual physical for your company. Stratagem does a check-up on every department and assesses how well it functions. Then we'll identify strengths, weaknesses, opportunities, threats, competitors and other factors that affect the health of your organization. Get ready to put pen to paper.

This comprehensive business evaluation is divided into six categories:
1. Sales and marketing
2. Production and services
3. People
4. Finance
5. Information systems
6. Location

The questions that follow are not necessarily a comprehensive list of all the questions relevant to your particular business. The facilitator, however, in their planning work will have considered the most relevant questions by editing the list that follows. The important objective in the Business Review section of the Stratagem meeting is to identify what needs to change to make it possible to achieve the vision and goals identified earlier in the meeting.

1. SALES AND MARKETING

First, let's define the market and your approach. From here, we'll refine the approach if it is too scattered and needs direction. For example, some possible approaches are to scattergun the entire market — or selectively market to each segment. You might consider niche marketing and focusing all of your efforts on one segment. This exercise will help you define your marketing universe so you can prioritize and plan.

Your Go-to-Market Approach

- What is your target market?
- What are the market segments?
- What is your marketing plan?
- What market research do you conduct — or what research are you planning on carrying out? How will this research be done?

Market Segment	Opportunities	Threats	Main Competitor
1.			
2.			
3.			
4.			
5.			

Your Competition

Now, let's take a serious look at who you are competing against. Consider your competitive edge — why do you ultimately gain the client? What seals the deal for your customers when they choose your company?

First begin by identifying key competitors:

Competitor	Position	Strengths	Weaknesses
1.			
2.			
3.			
4.			
5.			

Next, determine what differentiates your company from your competitors. More importantly, how does this benefit your clients? By going through this process, you will determine the unique perceived benefit of your company.

Complete the following statement for each of your company's competitive differentiators.

Only we: [insert differentiator]

Which means that: [how you act/conduct business as a cause of this]

Clients benefit because: [how clients realize the value of this differentiator]

Profile Your Customers

Let's closely analyze your current customer base. As you do this exercise, consider: Is your client list growing? Who is your ideal customer and how are you targeting this person/organization? What is your record of client retention? What is your customer target, and how will you achieve this?

Now, review the customers in your portfolio and determine the following:
- Top clients ranked by revenue generated.
- Top clients ranked by profitability.
- Clients with most cross-referral opportunities.
- Clients who are unprofitable.

Customer satisfaction: How do you monitor and follow up on positive and negative customer feedback?

Describe Your Sales Process

How do you turn those target customers into loyal clients? And, how long does it take you to convert a prospect into a customer? Let's take a look at your sales process.

- Who is on the sales team?
- What is the process for generating leads and managing the lead process?
- Do you reward sales staff for generating new business, and if so, how?
- How do you rate your overall sales process?
- What are the strengths of the process — where do you regularly find success?
- What is most frustrating about the sales process — what do you wish to improve?

Marketing Objectives

Consider how you go to market and what response you gain from these tactics. We're talking the whole marketing picture here — advertising, exhibitions, marketing collateral like brochures, leaflets, newsletters, online efforts (e-news, social media, and so on) seminars, direct mail and networking.

- What are your marketing goals and what are the timelines for these goals?
- Some examples:
  - *Sell 10 percent more services to existing clients within the year.*
  - *Expand the number of offices within 15 months.*
  - *Raise brand market share by 12 percent within 12 months.*

Your Marketing Plan

- Who is your marketing champion? Who directs, manages and implements the marketing strategy?

- Do you have a marketing plan, and what time frame does it cover (one year, 15 months, and so on)?
- How do you measure results?
- What is your marketing budget?
- Your marketing plan will consider and include details about:
  — Products and/or services.
  — Sales/distribution channels.
  — Price.
  — Promotion.

2. PRODUCTION AND SERVICES

Let's get back to your strategic objectives. Consider how the products and services you provide meet those objectives.

- Are there limits to your ability to produce more products or sell more services? If yes, why?

- How efficient is your current production system?

- Have you made the optimum use of technology in your processes?

- Describe your relationships with key suppliers.

- Which suppliers do you enjoy purchasing from? Why?

- What terms have you established with main suppliers?

- Do you have an alternative source of supply? Please describe.

- Do you review your overheads? How do they look?

- What is your work-in-progress policy?

- Do you outsource, and what is your process for doing so?

- Additional comments:

3. PEOPLE

Your team is paramount to the success of your company. They say you are only as strong as the weakest link on your team, and that is true. The team you build and nurture will execute the Stratagem plan. Let's take stock of the players today, potential skills gaps, incentives, training and other aspects of recruiting, raising and retaining a top-tier team.

- If you were not available for three months, how would your absence impact the business?

- Who, if anyone, is the business dependent on?

- What is your level of staff turnover?

- How do you incentivize staff?

- Describe your company's culture.

- Have you clearly defined your core values and how do you enforce them?

- Do you hold staff appraisals (performance reviews), and how are these conducted?

- Describe your training program.

- Describe your staff mix. Do you feel the mix is appropriate? Are there gaps, and if so, what skills are lacking?

- What is your health and safety policy?

- How do you keep up-to-date with current employment legislation?

- What is your recruitment plan for filling open positions?

- Additional comments:

4. FINANCE

The status of an organization's financial health will dictate its ability to fulfill goals and, ultimately, implement a strategic plan. Cash flow, debt, assets — where do you stand? Let's take a closer look at how your business is financed, how you are paid by your customers (and how quickly), and what you anticipate your funding requirement to be in the future.

- How is the business financed?

- Does the company have adequate finances to meet daily requirements for the next 12 months and beyond?

- How would additional financing be used in the business?

- Do your customers pay on time? What is the typical aging on accounts receivable?

- Do you pay suppliers on time? What is your average pay schedule?

- Do you have a business plan?

- Do you prepare regular cash flow forecasts?

- Do you maintain a strong relationship with your bank?

- What securities do your bankers hold?

- Does your business have surplus assets?

- Additional comments:

5. INFORMATION SYSTEMS

Technology is the lifeblood of a business today — the rapid, secure flow of information in and out of the business is critical for its success. And, the efficiency and effectiveness of information technology (IT) systems directly impact marketing, sales, production and every aspect of an organization. When is the last time you evaluated your IT portfolio? What information are your systems gathering/organizing and are they working at optimum speed? Let's take a closer look.

- Describe the IT systems you currently use.

- Do you get the information you want from these systems?

- What systems would improve your processes?

- Do you get information on time? Why or why not?

- How reliant is your business on IT?

- What is your IT contingency plan?

- Who maintains your IT systems?

- Who is responsible for IT systems in your company?

- How good is your website?

- Do you sell products or services online?

- What is your IT budget?

- How far ahead do you plan for changes in IT systems? What changes are you currently planning?

- When was the last time you had a professional review your IT systems?

- Additional comments:

6. LOCATION

The financing and functionality of your workspace directly affects productivity and your organization's ability to reach strategic objectives. This is true whether you operate out of a single office or headquarters, multiple locations or branches located all over the world. Let's take stock of your real estate, owned and leased, and how it works for your business.

- Where is your business located? Are you in the right location?

- Do you own or lease the premises?

- If owned, what is the current market value and amount of outstanding loans?

- If leased, when does the lease expire, or when is the next break?

- Does your facility meet your space requirements today? In five to ten years? Please describe.

- Additional comments:

Sterling Case 3: Pressing the Reset Button on Expectations

The world has changed drastically during the past several years. Sterling was playing a different game when the firm began its Stratagem process in 2010 — since that time, the business climate has continued its dynamic (and sometimes turbulent) path. Through Stratagem discussions, Kosoy recognized that educating Sterling's investors and partners was a critical step to building value in the organization.

"It became apparent that we needed to educate them as to what more realistic returns were going to look like going forward," Kosoy says. *"We felt we could still deliver excellent relative returns versus our peer group, but it would be extremely difficult to replicate the huge absolute returns of our past."*

That was OK, but it was time to press the reset button on expectations so investors and partners could think practically about outcomes. Three areas had to be clearly addressed:

- **Strengthening communication.** For investors to understand the steep shifts that had occurred in the real estate industry, Kosoy says the company needed to communicate clearly that it could continue to deliver solid absolute returns and excellent relative returns — but times were different. *"The shift in our world had to be communicated clearly, honestly and succinctly,"* he says.

- **Mixing institutional investors.** Moving toward a better mix of institutional investors, coupled with the firm's high-net worth group, the business would grow more stable. *"We believed there was a much better understanding and appreciation for relative returns in the institutional world, particularly in a tough and very fragile market,"* Kosoy says.

- **Securing capital.** Kosoy also recognized that Sterling would perform better for investors in relative and absolute terms if the firm gained access to fully discretionary capital. *"Securing that needed to be the top priority for our firm, and it needed to be executed in an expedited manner,"* Kosoy says.

Sterling Case 4: Letting Go

Stratagem can uncover personnel issues and that can result in tough decisions for owners. Kosoy shares how a longtime, non-senior management member of the team needed to find another opportunity outside of the organization. *"The friction between what was best for our business and the loyalty we felt we needed to show an individual who had been with us for many years led to many sleepless nights,"* Kosoy says.

Kosoy shares the weight of the decision …

"In a vibrant economy where jobs were aplenty, it would have been easy to make the human resources move we felt necessary. But in 2010, there were no jobs being created, and especially not in real estate. This compounded our concern for this person's post-Sterling job prospects. We were not sure where our colleague would find other work.

"But we had to cut this individual loose. Stratagem had made it clear that the employee had become an organizational cancer — far more than we realized or were prepared to admit to ourselves. We knew that in order to continue our growth journey, we had to fine-tune our team and align management and all employees toward our goals. By making this difficult personnel decision, we shed a weight that would have held back progressive change for our organization."

Chapter 7

Starco: A Case for Stratagem

Now that we have shown you how to plan and conduct a Stratagem meeting, let's take a look at a hypothetical case study that illustrates exactly how Stratagem can take your business to a higher level. We'll explore why a hypothetical company called Starco decided to implement Stratagem, how they prepared for the process, what happened during the meeting, and how the process resulted in actions, successes and a changed culture. Through this case, you will see how Stratagem can ignite a sea change within the organization — and why you should rethink the old way of strategic planning and start thinking the Stratagem way.

LOOKING FOR A NEW WAY TO STRATEGIZE

Starco is a manufacturer of cleaning chemicals for the food manufacturing industry based in Maryland that has annual sales revenue of $32 million, employs 200 people and is a third-generation, family-owned business. The company's executives include a husband and wife team and trusted managers with tenure. They've mostly grown up in the organization and are family, too. Every year, the management team dedicates a full day to planning the upcoming year. They call it strategic planning, but for the most part, these meetings end up being a forum for airing grievances over particular processes. Sure, large goals are discussed, but there is no deep digging or assigning tasks to begin reaching those goals. Someone takes notes, a document is produced, and it essentially collects dust until the next year's meeting.

Bill Owers, 58, is the chairman and CEO of the company. Bill is the grandson of the founder of the business and he also owns a majority of the company's voting stock. He started working full time at the company after he left high school. Following a health scare, he is seriously considering his longer term options for himself and the business, however, he has never really seen an alternative to him continuing to work because who else would lead the business? There is no family succession in the business as his son is an oil executive in Houston and his daughter is a lawyer in New York. Neither have shown any interest in coming back to Maryland to get involved in the family business. Bill's wife, Judy, has played a supporting role to the sales director but has assisted Bill with various aspects of running the business over the years. For most of his life, the business has kept Bill anchored close to home but he and his wife want to be able to explore the world. The problem is, he realized that his business practices — delegating was always a problem for him, as was planning for the future — would never allow him to realize his personal goals to travel and enjoy leisure time in retirement. He recognized that a new type of planning was necessary, but what?

Bill had heard a friend talk about Stratagem and what it had done for their business. He decided to give this holistic, practical strategic planning method a shot. After all, his annual meetings were not producing results, and aside from a week or two of feeling charged up, the other managers fast forgot any discussions that took place behind closed doors. Business always continued as usual.

Bill recognized that in order for him to reach his personal goals he needed to focus on developing his senior management team and on passing the baton. The business needed to learn to function without him. So, HR processes were necessary: policies, procedures, getting best practices down on paper such that they had hired their first HR director in the last six months. Because the closely held family business had run on trust and handshakes for so many years, many of these formalities had been overlooked. Bill knew he would be tied down to the business until the business could run without him at the helm. It was time to take action.

Bill therefore decided to try Stratagem. He considered whether he could take on the role of mediator/facilitator at the Stratagem meeting — and certainly, he could have taken this approach — but he decided that he really needed to find someone who could facilitate and oversee the process. The facilitator would coach managers through the Stratagem session and act as a referee on the sidelines, making sure that the meeting progressed in a productive and constructive manner. The facilitator would also make sure that the participants successfully completed all the steps of the Stratagem process and ensure that individuals were allocated responsibility for each action point and a realistic deadline for implementation for each action point was set. The organization could not afford to spend another year drafting a shelf document that lacked assigned action steps.

WHO SHOULD FACILITATE? WHO SHOULD ATTEND?

Bill really thought long and hard about whom should attend the Stratagem session. Certainly Judy needed to be there given the importance of the decisions facing Bill and the business.

But who else?

Starco's day-to-day management team comprised:
Bill Owers (age 58) – CEO
John Brady (age 60) – Production Director
Sally Jansen (age 41) – HR Director
Tom Melvin (age 46) – Financial Director
Jim Fitzpatrick (age 51) – Sales Director

Bill felt uneasy about Jim's long-term loyalty to the business and they had experienced a number of heated exchanges in recent months as Bill had felt Jim was chasing sales at the expense of margin. Jim felt Bill was trying to micro-manage the sales function. Bill just wasn't sure whether Jim would contribute constructively at the Stratagem session and whether his presence might be disruptive. He knew that the others in the senior management team really cared about the business although some issues facing the business were, in Bill's opinion, caused by some of the behaviors and actions of the senior management team. Bill knew that his senior management team saw him as a micro-manager who wanted to interfere in all their respective functions. Also, Tom had only been with the business for six months and Bill wondered if he would be in a position to add much to the discussion.

Bill thought this might all be too difficult and maybe it was best that only he and Judy attend the Stratagem session on their own. However, the key people who drive the business on a day-to-day basis wouldn't be there, so how could they hold a really meaningful session. Would the others buy in to what they decided?

Bill decided to do two things. First, he spoke to Judy about what she thought. She thought Stratagem sounded like a good thing to do, something that could really help their business. Next, thinking of a potential facilitator, he called his longtime CPA and adviser, Don

Andrew and asked for Don's opinion on who should attend and whether Don would be prepared to facilitate the Stratagem session.

Don immediately thought Stratagem was a great idea especially as he and Bill had various conversations on key strategic issues over the years but they had never done it in as structured a way as Stratagem offered. Don's suggestion to Bill was that the Stratagem session should be facilitated by Karen Armenti, one of Don's partners who was more experienced in facilitating group discussions and, if Bill was agreeable, that Don sit in on the session, too, just to observe and take notes. Bill agreed with this approach.

On the important question of who should attend, Don and Bill debated the merits of the various combinations. They decided that if they were going to move the business forward, Bill needed to trust and be open with his senior management team. If he couldn't trust them, whom could he trust? If Jim was difficult to work with during the session, then the presence of the rest of the group should temper any challenging situation. And, having the group involved would be important so conclusions could be made about Jim's performance and ability to work as a team. Ultimately, Bill, Judy and the entire senior management team would attend Stratagem, with Karen as facilitator and Don in attendance — just the combination Judy had suggested when Bill first asked for her input.

INFO GATHERING

Bill collected the background materials Karen needed to properly facilitate the meeting. This allowed her to prep so that valuable time during the Stratagem session was not spent digesting background information about the business and its performance. Participants were given a flavor of the process and also asked to consider their own business and personal goals in advance.

In effect, there is very little preparation that any of the participants have to do in advance of the day except have an open mind and be prepared to switch off from day-to-day operational activities. The facilitator does the real preparation work, because they need to know the background and have a flavor of the big issues.

Bill compiled copies of the following information for the facilitator in advance of the Stratagem session:

- Most recent annual audited financial statements.
- Most recent management accounts.
- The people organization chart including titles, duties and years of service.
- The chart of the legal structure of the business and details of shareholdings.
- Copies of any recent strategic or business plan documents.
- List from CEO of what he sees as the biggest issues facing the business (the facilitator will keep this list confidential).
- Literature explaining what the business does (the facilitator will also have a good look at the company's website).
- Breakdown of the last two years' sales by value and customer.
- Financial forecast for current year.

SETTING THE TONE FOR CHANGE

Bill decided they would hold the Stratagem session off-site at a hotel conference room, outside Maryland so he and his team could really feel they were switching off from the work at the factory. Bill did consider some alternatives — meeting at a local park pavilion, for example. But he figured this environment would not create the same inspiring atmosphere to really think about the future for themselves and the business.

A few weeks before the Stratagem session, Karen drafted a memo for Bill to distribute to all the participants explaining more about what the Stratagem session was all about and that she would facilitate with Don present. The memo reminded everyone of the atmosphere of openness and trust encouraging everyone to participate actively and constructively. The memo explained that the purpose of the day was not to go into territory that anyone was uncomfortable venturing into but that it was important for the business and individuals that important issues were addressed.

Bill's memo set out a few ground rules. For one, no cell phone use aside from a few allotted breaks to check email. The dress code would be business casual and everything to be discussed was strictly confidential unless they all agreed that certain points discussed should be communicated to other people in the organization.

Everyone understood that the meeting would result in various action steps and that each participant would be held accountable for implementing aspects of the company's Stratagem plan. This was to be a team effort and would require full participation and commitment from every participant.

Because of thorough preparation and advance communication, Bill and his senior management team were excited about the prospect of the Stratagem day and they only had to get themselves sufficiently organized to be able to get out of the office for the day without worrying what was happening back at home base.

As it transpired, this first Stratagem session was the beginning of some significant changes at Starco — a way of melding personal and business goals, defining objectives, assigning roles, and executing on the vision so the company and its players could realize desired results.

If honest with himself, Bill certainly was initially skeptical and anxious that Stratagem would change much about the business but when his whole management team bought into the idea, Bill knew this was going to be different.

A Clear Mind

The marriage of personal and business goals is what differentiates Stratagem from most other strategic planning methodologies. Stratagem is not complex, nor does it employ complicated formulas. It does not require a third-party facilitator, though Starco decided that bringing in a professional to lead the session was the best way to proceed. Stratagem, as a process, is simple. What's critical, as Bill realized, is ensuring that the agreed action plan is properly allocated and people are accountable for their action points.

In the case of Starco, because Bill had taken no steps to create a succession plan, there was much to do. Rather than do too much thinking in advance of the Stratagem session, Bill decided to do exactly what the Stratagem process suggests — turn up with a clear mind, no preconceived agenda, and be prepared to discuss and share personal and business goals. The power of doing this spontaneously and in a trusted group during Stratagem cannot be underestimated. This is one of the real powers of the process.

THE STRATAGEM DAY

Arriving at the Mayflower Hotel at 9 a.m. on the day of the session, Bill, Judy and the senior management team were welcomed by Karen and Don. This was followed by coffee and a relaxing chat among themselves, where everyone could be introduced to each other.

Laid out on the table were the Stratagem participant workbooks with the name of each participant on a cover so each person knew where to sit. Don was sitting quietly at the back of the room and Bill immediately noticed that Judy was opposite him, and, to her right next to where Karen was standing was Jim. He could see that Karen had put some thought into the seating plan!

Karen set the tone by welcoming everyone and reminding them of the key points included in Bill's earlier *setting the scene* memo. Karen emphasized the importance of thinking openly and constructively about the business and themselves. She reminded everyone that she would not take anyone to a place they didn't want to go and that if there was an issue that was particularly delicate then the issue might be parked to be revisited at a later stage. She equally reminded everyone that there is no time deadline to a Stratagem session — it will finish when it naturally finishes and it will be obvious when that point is, but that could be 4 p.m. or it could be midnight! She did promise, to everyone's relief though, that they would have regular breaks throughout the day.

With the scene and the ground rules now set, Karen turned to her first PowerPoint slide and Starco's first Stratagem day was underway. Everyone shared some nervousness but the overwhelming emotion was excitement as to what the day ahead would reveal and the change that would result from the whole team being open and engaging in the future strategy for themselves and the business in this way. The senior management team was particularly interested in hearing what Bill and Judy's plans were for the business.

The Outcome

Starco had a hugely constructive day and despite Bill's fears about his attitude, Jim made a valuable contribution and the air was cleared time and time again. Karen tactfully pried out of the group the thorny issues but always knew when to gently back off when the going got heated.

The group was stunned but very excited when Bill announced during the session — with guidance and support from Judy and Don — that he really wanted to sell the business in the next three years to the management team. A lot of the discussion focused round what the business needed to do to get it into the position so that the buy-out would succeed including funding and agreeing on who Bill's successor would be. These were deep but critical issues and Karen kept the discussion on track. The weaknesses Bill saw in some of his colleagues and the business were openly discussed and the day resulted in each of them having a much better understanding of what was important to each individual and therefore what as a group they were aiming for.

Beyond that big issue, the group also agreed on an exciting vision for the business, which was to become a top five player in the manufacture and supply of cleaning chemicals for the food industry in the U.S. It was ambitious but achievable. The group spent a large part of the Stratagem day discussing exactly what they would need to do to achieve that vision and they dissected Starco piece by piece and agreed on what needed to be fixed — from people to finance to production — to make the business stronger and capable of achieving the goals they set as part of the journey to their vision.

By 6:30 p.m. Karen could see the participants were exhausted and they had upturned every conceivable stone about their own goals and the business. Don had taken copious pages of notes, which Karen and he could now use to write up the strategic plan for Starco.

Karen summarized the finding of the day by running through the key points she had noted on the two flip charts she used. For the first time Starco had articulated its vision, Bill had made the major decision about how and when he and Judy would exit the business and there were pages of action points all with allocated responsibilities and timescales.

Yes the group was exhausted, but the overwhelming sense was one of exhilaration and excitement about the future of the business and for themselves. Not only did each participant know what he or she wanted that future to look like but they were now clear about what was expected of them in playing their role to make that future a reality.

Karen asked each participant at the table for their views on the day. Their feedback reinforced the value each person had received from the day and showed Bill that he had a management team that was capable of taking the business to the next level. He was glad he had taken the plunge and agreed to hold a Stratagem session. Looking at her husband from across the table, there was no one happier than Judy.

The plan was set and now the action would begin.

ONE-WEEK LATER AND FOLLOW UP

A week after Starco's Stratagem day, a large package arrived on Bill's desk. Inside he found a copy of Starco's strategic plan written by Karen and Don, listing the vision, the strategic goals and the detailed action points by area. Bill skimmed through it and could see that it was a full record of all the decisions and action points. His eye caught the action points with his name next to them as the person responsible for their implementation. He also saw in the package that there was a sealed envelope for him. The envelope contained his own personal copy of his workbook with his responses to the questions on personal and business goals, which had been openly shared with the group during the Stratagem session. There were also sealed private and confidential envelopes containing the personal workbooks for all the other participants including their copy of the full strategic plan. Bill had thought a lot about the content of the Stratagem day in the week since and it was good to have the written record that they could now use to monitor progress on their plans.

Bill decided that he would check in regularly with each manager and find out whether progress was being made to reach the relevant goal. Regular group email exchanges would also help keep the team on task. Bill also decided that the group would reconvene each quarter for a couple of hours to discuss progress and hash through challenges. It had been a good day out of the office discussing the big picture and now they had a clear plan. Bill was determined the Stratagem report would not gather dust; Stratagem was evolving from a meeting into a mind-set.

REVISITING STRATAGEM

The next year, when Starco's senior management team convened for their second Stratagem meeting, again facilitated by Karen, they reviewed the status of the previous year's goals. The company was building — truly moving forward on a large-scale plan to create an organization that was not dependent on Bill and one where the management buy-out was close to becoming a reality. Bill had even been on a previously unheard of week-long trip and checked in periodically via email. It was the first time he left town and actually took the whole planned vacation. In the past, he always returned early to put out a fire or attend a meeting. Something always disrupted his personal time. He was beginning to achieve a balance he never thought possible.

Of course, all of this was work in progress. But Starco took a big leap in one year. The management team felt recharged because they, too, were working toward aligned business and personal goals. The company was functioning as an engine with many moving parts working together as opposed to a train running full speed ahead with a single conductor behind the wheel.

At the third annual Stratagem session, Bill announced that the time to effect the buy-out was now. Tom had been grooming a financial controller who was ready to step up to the senior management team and the others were unanimous that Tom should become the new CEO upon Bill's retirement. The balance sheet was strong and the marketing plan hatched at the first Stratagem session showed that while there was still some way to go, the business was well on its way to achieving its vision.

Stratagem hadn't provided the answers for Bill and his team — the answers came from within. However, Stratagem created the environment where finding the answers became possible. It also meant that management felt more empowered, more valued. And the organization is stronger and more profitable because of the more cohesive culture.

Chapter 8

Building the Strategic Plan

Think about the last strategic plan you created for your company, assuming you have ever done this. Now ask yourself these questions: Did the plan assign specific responsibilities? How often did you revisit and update the plan? Did the document address business goals while considering life goals? Is the plan relevant today?

A strategic plan should grow with your company — it is a measuring stick for success, but only if it is treated as a living document.

In Chapter 6 you spent some time seriously analyzing your organization by completing a business review. You are now prepared to put pen to paper to begin building the strategic plan. The plan culminates your vision, core values and goals. It addresses the strengths and weaknesses you examined during the detailed business review and it pinpoints opportunities for growth, increased profits and succession.

One of the key differences between a Stratagem plan and other strategic plans — the ones that are likely collecting dust on a shelf — is the usability of the Stratagem plan. By this, we mean that it serves as much more than a thesis on what the company should do to succeed. The Stratagem plan is an action plan that doles out responsibility. It addresses who will do what. It sets time marker goals. It includes the all-important accountability factor.

Another thing about the Stratagem plan — its relevant components should be shared with appropriate parties. It should not remain in hiding in the boardroom, where only top executives are privy to its contents. We're not suggesting you copy and hand out the plan to every person at your company. But you should consider coaching key leaders on the parts of the plan that apply to their departments. Then, they must convey those goals and action steps to their employees, giving them an idea of how their role fits into the big picture. Otherwise how will the CFO reach his or her department-specific goals if his or her team is not aware of them? As we noted earlier, when workers realize their jobs contribute significantly to the company's purpose and mission, they approach their roles with a sense of pride and ownership. This attitude is contagious in an organization, and it's exactly what you need to successfully implement a Stratagem plan.

STRATEGIC PLAN FRAMEWORK

The information and issues you shared about your company during the business review provide a lot of the detail of the strategic plan. In other words, having set your vision, your personal and business goals, the big question is how are you going to make this all happen in practice. Is the current structure and shape of the business fit for the purpose and ambitions you have set?

In the business review, you addressed six areas: sales and marketing, production and services, people, finance, information systems and location. During those exercises, you examined competitors, profiled customers and set objectives in those key areas, from marketing to IT. Now, it's time to synthesize that information and pour it into a strategic plan the Stratagem way. The strategic plan you create will help align your organization and help you better manage market turbulence.

Your plan will not look like any other. We cannot provide you a fill-in-the-blanks template. Rather, you'll apply the intelligence you uncovered during the Stratagem session and address these key subject areas in the plan:

- Vision Statement: What do you want the business to look like when you are finished?
- Strategic Goals: On your journey towards your vision, what short-term and medium-term goals are you setting for yourself and the business?
- Business Review: To achieve your vision and strategic goals, what action needs to happen in each area of the business to make this possible?
- Action: Allocating responsibility and a timescale to achieve implementation of each action point.

Implementing the Plan

The power of putting a plan on paper is that all of the information collected during the business review and discussed during Stratagem sessions becomes real. It's there, right in front of you. And, frankly, you can't ignore it. In a sense, the written strategic plan is a contract binding your management team to the goals they have set. It holds parties responsible for executing on the mission. If you treat the plan this way, it will certainly serve as that living document and maintain its relevance. The strategic plan is not a message in a bottle — a great dream you send out to sea. It should be an everyday document that leaders in the organization can refer to often as they work to reach goals.

What we are saying is, you can't just write the plan. You must implement it. After you go through the labor of creating the plan, you are left with the job of executing on it. But how does this happen?

When a strategic plan includes these components, it becomes an actionable plan that can be realistically implemented. For each goal set in the plan, consider these three points:
- Measurable objectives: How will you measure the success?
- Specific timetables: When should the goal(s) be completed?
- Responsible parties: Who will be in charge of making sure objectives are carried out?

Sterling Case 5: Revisiting Stratagem

How often should you conduct a Stratagem session? What's necessary to keep the process fresh and active in your organization? How do you ensure that the goals you set during the meeting are executed?

Accountability is a key part of Stratagem and what separates this method of strategic planning from the old way. By assigning tasks to individuals and measuring progress, companies are able to realize the goals they set. For example, Kosoy says Sterling successfully executed on 90 percent of what the firm identified during its Stratagem session. Of the remaining 10 percent, 5 percent of the goals were not pursued because of market conditions, and the other 5 percent the firm simply failed to get done. Kosoy says this is in no part due to the failure of anyone in the organization.

On an irregular basis, Kosoy and his partner review their Stratagem plan and review where they wanted to go, taking an inventory of accomplishments. They ask, *"What could we have done better? Why did we decide not to pursue a certain strategy?"* Kosoy confirms, *"Stratagem has clearly become an integral part of our firm's long-term planning culture."*

Still, Kosoy recognizes that the first Stratagem sessions for Sterling were conducted in 2010. A lot has changed since then. *"It's once again time to get out of the weeds, stand back, push forward, strategize, focus, outline and pursue an extended vision for the future of our firm,"* he says.

Kosoy and his team will regroup to participate in another Stratagem session, three years following their first. *"When we were approached to try Stratagem two years ago, the thought was that we had nothing to lose by participating,"* Kosoy says. *"Today, we believe that there is potentially much more to lose by not participating in the process."*

Chapter 9

The Stratagem Habit

Stratagem is much more than a process for holding a strategic planning meeting and writing a plan. It's a mind-set. Stratagem changes the way you think about your business and life. It marries these worlds so you can set goals that will truly allow you to reach your professional and personal dreams. We realize this sounds like a lofty claim — but companies who have implemented Stratagem and embrace it as part of their culture attest to the power of this thinking.

Stratagem becomes a habit and way of doing business when the process is infused into a company's culture. Stratagem sessions should occur as often as the company needs to continue seeing through its strategic plan, continuing to infuse, revise and adjust as circumstances require (change in personnel, winning new customers, adding new product lines, and so on). Further, working with a facilitator to implement Stratagem builds further accountability. The facilitator is able to check in regularly to see how the plan is working for the business, discusses obstacles and guides the organization toward solutions to keep the plan running smoothly.

A 4-Point Plan — Make Stratagem A Habit In Your Firm:

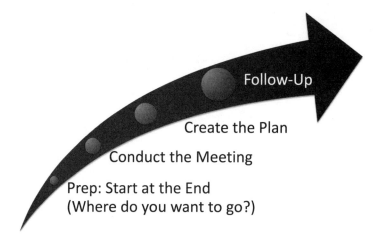

Follow-Up

Create the Plan

Conduct the Meeting

Prep: Start at the End
(Where do you want to go?)

Revisit the Plan: The group who set the plan should meet and review its contents every three months. Set time aside during a board or management meeting to accomplish this — build it into your existing meeting structure so this important task does not get pushed aside: 1. Discuss the plan and progress made; 2. Identify and address obstacles; 3. Hash through solutions; 4. Share successes.

Adopt a Mentor: Who in the organization is responsible for delivering the plan? In most cases, it is the organization's CEO. This person should be mentored by a person who can hold them accountable for executing the plan, and provide continuous support and guidance during the journey to achieve the company's goals.

Produce a Summary: Distill the strategic plan into a single-page document, then laminate this and share it with everyone in the organization. This creates accountability and fosters a sense of ownership of the plan. It takes the plan from seeming like a big secret to an exciting venture that everyone will take part in to help the company grow and thrive. Everyone holds a piece of the plan and contributes to the transformation.

Schedule Stratagem Update Sessions: For example, plan every year for a Stratagem update session, where you'll review the success of the current plan and edit it to retain its relevancy.

Sterling Case 6: Success with Stratagem

In many ways, your business is like a child. The time devoted, emotions invested, the relationships grown over time — we do all we can to protect this very personal part of who we are, what we stand for. But as Kosoy shares, this very perspective can prevent us from honest strategic planning. Stratagem helps bring tough situations to the surface in an environment where issues and solutions are addressed.

The key is to let go and allow the process to unfold, he says. The more you guard your baby during Stratagem, the less effective the process will be. By opening up and answering the tough questions, really seeing your business for what and "who" it is, you will have great success with the process.

Let your guard down. *"Many who run businesses don't want to hear about or deal with their weaknesses and prefer to focus on their strengths,"* Kosoy says. *"They particularly don't want to hear about areas of improvement from a third-party who isn't living and breathing the business every minute."* But this objective third-party helps the team open up.

✓ Allow a third-party to facilitate the Stratagem session.

✓ Allow uncomfortable issues to rise to the surface — don't fight it.

✓ Listen. Give everyone involved the necessary airtime to express their views.

✓ Take the opportunity during your Stratagem session to confront matters that have been festering in the organization. *"You will get more out of the process if you submit freely to it,"* Kosoy advises.

Tap the opportunity to improve. *"We can all improve in every aspect of our lives as people and as businesses and we should work to constantly do so,"* Kosoy says. Contentment feels great, but it's not going to foster growth or innovation. *"Check your ego at the door."* And Kosoy recommends not limiting too greatly the topics you'll address during your Stratagem session. *"Be prepared to focus on the personal just as much as the professional. These goals are equally important."*

Create a safe environment. Every team member involved should feel comfortable saying anything and everything they think and feel. *"Everyone needs to feel safe, participating with little risk of being placed on the defensive,"* Kosoy says. *"You will get a ton out of the process if you step back and listen to what your teammates are saying. Really hear them and absorb fully what is being said, how it is being said, and what is truly meant."*

Everything to gain. *"Everyone is built differently and needs to be managed differently to achieve maximum productivity, personal satisfaction and happiness, which all lead to a successful business,"* Kosoy says. *"Remember with Stratagem that you have nothing to lose, and everything to gain."*

Sterling Case 7: A Stratagem Culture, By Nature

Kosoy did not want Stratagem to be jammed down the throats of his management team. That wasn't the idea at all. Rather, the method provided a platform for uncovering some real issues in the organization and a forum for identifying solutions.

There was no reason to force the system into the daily routine. After engaging in the Stratagem process, Kosoy says, the two-day, intensive session keenly focused his team. The effects were long-lasting and made an imprint on how the organization conducts strategic planning. In fact, Kosoy says, *"The results were longer-lasting and more permanent than I believed they would be."*

It evolved naturally as a by-product of the hard work and goals set during the Stratagem sessions. *"We all just got it and began rowing in unison, in the same direction, with a laser focus on our goals, and we have continued to do so,"* Kosoy shares.

Stratagem soaked into the culture without Kosoy or Sterling's managers forcing it into the stream of business. And this is best, Kosoy says, because it's simply not productive to force people to act in a programmed way. *"I have long believed that general individual human nature is very hard to change, and sustaining non-natural behavior over an extended period of time for an individual is not only draining, but almost impossible without significantly impacting the contentment and internal satisfaction of the individual,"* he says. As an example, a big-picture thinker can drill down and focus only on details for so long. *"They will ultimately revert to their big-picture ways because that's who they are.*

"While our firm's culture and soul remains unchanged, I believe that as a team we have changed significantly over the past two years, with no risk to reversion in sight," he says. *"Perhaps it was new team members that changed the dynamics, or our increased size. Perhaps it is the keenly in-tuned group's mutual reliance on one another that is filling the gaps as members grab hold of areas in which they excel. Regardless, we know that Stratagem played a significant role in this cultural change."*

Conclusion

We opened the book talking about a new process for planning your business and your life. In Stratagem, we have developed and proved that this process works in a way that gives businesses a plan for growth without owners/executives having to sacrifice their personal lives as the offset cost for that growth. We believe we have demonstrated that leaders of organizations can strike that sought-after work/life balance. You can put time and energy into your business without taking it away from your personal life.

By regularly working the Stratagem process, you can create nimble long-range plans that are adaptable to unforeseen conditions in your market space. When this type of planning becomes a habit, it melds into your business structure: It becomes a tool and practice your leaders can rely on as they seek direction and insight on business and life.

We hope this book provides you with clarity on how you can take a fresh approach to strategic planning using a method that considers your whole life: business and personal. Stratagem works for your business whether your goals are to develop a plan that is transformational (to achieve rapid growth or succession) or targeted (become a top five player in your region). Stratagem's process and tools will provide your organization with an outlook and means to achieve whatever vision and ambitions you are willing to put on paper, as long as you are honest, open and willing to hold yourself accountable to make them happen!

So, are you ready to get started?

BY SANDY MANSON, JAY NISBERG AND GARY SHAMIS

APPENDIX I

THE
STRATAGEM
PROCESS

| Preparation: Start at the End | Conduct The Meeting | Create the Plan | Follow-Up Activity |

Steps:
- What are the key objectives for the Stratagem meeting?
- Who will attend?
- Who will facilitate?
- Which venue?
- Which subjects are out of bounds?
- Complete background research and information gathering (facilitator).
- Communicate to all participants the format of the Stratagem meeting.

Items to address during the meeting:
- Personal goals.
- Vision.
- Business goals.
- Business review.
- Capture key findings and decisions as basis for strategic plan.

- Document the key points arising from the Stratagem meeting, including the agreed vision, goals and action points.

- Distribute the written strategic plan to all relevant persons.
- Agree on follow-up action(s) to review progress with plan.

APPENDIX II

THE STRATAGEM WORKBOOK

Workbook Contents

1. Background

2. Personal Goals

3. Business Goals

4. Business Review

   4.1 Sales and Marketing

   4.2 Production and Services

   4.3 People

   4.4 Finance

   4.5 Information System

   4.6 Location

1. Background

- Financial Results
  — Prepare a pack that sets out the historic and forecast financial performance and position?

- Legal Structure
  — From what we know.

- Personnel
  — From what we know.

- Brief History
  — From what we know.

Confirm these points and move on.

2. Personal Goals

Name: _____

Age: _____

Role: _____

Years in current position: _____

- What motivated you to get into business?

- The thing you most enjoy about your current role is:

- Are you happy with your current role?

- If you had a magic wand, what would you change about your current role?

- The balance between work and home is:
    - ☐ About right
    - ☐ Work too hard
    - ☐ Could take on more challenging work

Comments:

- How successful do you feel? *(0 = low, 10 = high)*
  Score: _____

- What keeps you awake at night?

- What are your plans and thoughts on an eventual exit from or succession in the business?

- At what age would you like to retire?

- Do you regularly review your own personal financial plans?

• Additional comments:

3. Business Goals

• Where do you want the business to be in five years?

• What are the priorities for the business?

- If you had a magic wand, what would you change that would have the biggest positive impact on your business?

- What are your thoughts on the current level of bank borrowings?

- How dependent is the business on you?
  - ☐ Not at all
  - ☐ Fairly
  - ☐ Totally

- Do you have succession plans in place for transfer of ownership?

- Do you have succession plans in place for key positions?

- How motivated do you think the company's employees are? (0 = low, 10 = high)

    Current _____   Target _____

- What changes do you see in your industry?

- What is the potential for new products and services?

- How should you measure the success of your business?

- Which factors, if any, are holding you back from reaching your business goals?

- Do you have a structured sales and marketing plan?

- What changes would you make to your sales and marketing activities?

- Additional comments:

4. Business Review

4.1 SALES AND MARKETING

The market — your approach
• What is your target market, and how does it break down?

• What is your marketing plan?

- What market research do you carry out/are you planning to carry out and how will this be done?

The purpose is to examine your approach and refine if appropriate:

Market Segment	Opportunities	Threats	Main Competitor

Possible approaches:
- Scattergun to the whole market.
- Selective marketing with offerings to each segment.
- Niche marketing, concentrating all efforts on one segment.

• Additional comments:

Competitor Analysis

Competitor	Position	Strengths	Weaknesses

Other factors to consider

Competitive edge — what is the important X factor that differentiates your business?

- What makes your business different and more importantly, how does this benefit your clients? This process will help you to determine the unique perceived benefit. Consider:

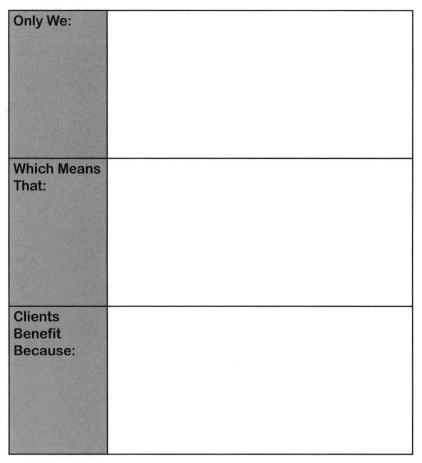

Only We:	
Which Means That:	
Clients Benefit Because:	

Customer portfolio review

Review customers within your portfolio and analyze to determine:
- Top clients ranked by revenue generated
- Top clients ranked by profitability
- Clients for cross-selling opportunities
- List clients who are regularly 'entertained' and identify gaps/over attention
- Is your client list growing? What is your target and how will you reach it?

What is your record of client retention?
- What is your target and how will you achieve this?

How do you currently identify and rate opportunities?
- How do you plan to exploit each opportunity?

• What steps need to be set in place to achieve your aim?

Describe your sales process
• Who is on the sales team?

• What is the process for generating sales leads and managing the lead process?

- Do you reward sales staff for generating new business?
  — What format does this take?

  — How successful is this process?

How do you monitor and measure customer satisfaction?
- Is there a process in place to follow up on positive and negative responses?

- What is your target and how will it be achieved?

Marketing objectives

What are your marketing goals and within what timescale?
For example:

- Sell 10 percent more services to existing clients within the year.
- Expand the number of offices within the next 15 months.
- Raise brand market share by 12 percent within 12 months.

Is marketing planned?

- Who is your marketing champion? Who directs and manages the marketing strategy and implementation of activity?

- Do you have a marketing plan and for what timeframe does it cover?

- How do you measure results?

- What is your marketing budget?
  Your marketing plan will consider and include details about:
      — Your products and/or services.
      — The place in which you sell them and other sales/
        distribution channels.
      — The price you charge for them.
      — The promotion you undertake.

- Do you review your range of marketing tactics?
  (Advertising, exhibitions, marketing collateral — brochures,
  leaflets, newsletters, seminars, PR, direct mail, Internet,
  networking)

Other considerations:
- *Financial investment.*
- *Staff resources — are their recruitment implications?*
- *Training.*
- *Organizational changes.*

4.2 PRODUCTION AND SERVICES

How do these fit your strategic objectives?
Points for consideration:
  • Are there limits to your ability to produce more product or sell more services? If yes, why?

  • How efficient is your current production system?

- Have you made the optimum use of technology in your processes?

- Do you have good relationships with your key suppliers?

- Which suppliers do you enjoy purchasing from? Why?

- What terms have you established with main suppliers?

- Do you have alternative sources of supply? Please describe.

- Do you review your overheads? How do they look?

- What is your work-in-progress policy?

- Do you outsource? What is your process for doing so?

- Additional comments:

4.3 PEOPLE

How do these fit your strategic objectives?
Points for consideration:

- What would be the impact on the business if you were not available for three months?

- Who, if anyone, is the business dependent on?

- What is your level of staff turnover?

- Do you have staff incentive schemes?

- Describe your company's culture:

- Have you clearly defined your core values and how do you enforce them?

- Do you hold staff appraisals?

- Do you have a staff training program?

• Do you have the correct staff mix?

• Do you have a health and safety policy?

• How do you keep up-to-date with current
  employment legislation?

- If filling vacancies is a difficult area, do you have a recruitment plan?

- Additional comments:

4.4 FINANCE

How do these fit your strategic objectives?
Points for consideration:

• How is the business financed?

• Does the company have adequate finances to meet daily requirements for the next 12 months and beyond?

• How would additional financing be used in the business?

- Do your customers pay on time? What is the typical aging on accounts receivable?

- Do you pay suppliers on time? What is your average pay schedule?

- Do you have a business plan?

• Do you prepare regular cash flow forecasts?

• Do you have a strong relationship with your bank?

• What securities do your bankers hold?

- Does the business have surplus assets?

- Additional comments:

4.5 INFORMATION SYSTEMS

How do these fit your strategic objectives?
Points for consideration:

• Describe the IT systems you currently use:

• Do you get the information you want from these systems?

- What systems would improve your processes?

- Do you get information on time? Why or why not?

- How reliant is your business on IT?

• What is your IT contingency plan?

• Who maintains your IT systems?

• Who is responsible for IT systems in your company?

- How good is your website?

- Do you sell products or services online?

- What is your IT budget?

- How far ahead do you plan changes in IT systems? What changes are you currently planning?

- When was the last time you had a professional review your IT systems?

- Additional comments:

4.6 LOCATION

How do these fit your strategic objectives?
Points for consideration:

- Where is your business located? Are you in the right
  location?

- Do you own or lease the premises?

- If owned, what is the current market value and amount of outstanding loans?

- Does your facility meet your space requirements today? In five to ten years? Please describe.

- Additional comments:

About the Authors:

Sandy Manson

Sandy Manson studied business and accountancy at the University of Edinburgh before training and qualifying as a Chartered Accountant with Arthur Andersen, where he worked in Edinburgh, London and Zurich. In 1991 he joined Johnston Carmichael, Scotland's largest independent firm of Chartered Accountants and business advisers and the creators of Stratagem. He was appointed CEO in 2007.

Sandy advises private corporations in a wide variety of industries and has extensive experience and expertise in strategic planning.

Jay Nisberg

Jay Nisberg is an internationally known management consultant recognized for his work in strategic planning and growth management with professional services firms and privately owned businesses. He is a frequent speaker at international conferences on topics such as executive leadership, strategic thinking and communications skills building. Jay is a noted author having published numerous articles on leadership and management. Jay is the author of *The Random House Handbook of Business Terms* as well as *The Random House Dictionary of Business Terms*. He co-authored the book, *How To Manage Your Accounting Practice: Taking Your Firm from Chaos to Consensus*. Jay's areas of expertise include strategic thinking and planning, as well as mergers and acquisitions. He is a leading expert on executive coaching and has consulted professional services firms including law and CPA firms, General Motors, RCA Corp. and the White House. He is frequently quoted in professional journals, newspapers and reference materials.

For the past twenty years Jay has been honored by *Accounting Today*, an industry news magazine, as the longest active member of their "Top 100 Most Influential People in the Accounting Profession," longer than any other individual on the list. As president of his own management consulting firm, he has advised businesses and professional firms around the world. He founded the Professionals Alliance Group focused on managing client assets and sits on the advisory boards of several of his clients.

Jay resides in Palm Beach, Florida with his wife Sally Ann. He can be reached best by email at jaynisberg@snet.net.

Gary Shamis

As managing director, Gary Shamis is responsible for day-to-day management at SS&G, a Top 40 US accounting firm. He chairs the firm's executive committee, which leads SS&G's strategy and growth initiatives. Gary is the recipient of numerous awards for growth and innovation. He is an author, speaker, instructor and adviser on myriad accounting and management topics. Gary is an active board member to several nonprofits, and the founder and chairman emeritus of LEA Global.

He earned his master's in accountancy from The Ohio State University and his bachelor of science from Tulane University.